PERFECTION LEARNING®

Who Gets More?

Allyson Valentine Schrier

Table of Contents

1

Pizza for Two

Ding-dong. The pizza is
here! It needs to be sliced.

Two people, one pizza.

Cut it down the middle. Now there are two equal pieces. Each piece is one-half of the whole pizza. One-half is written like this: $\frac{1}{2}$.

Each slice of pizza is a **fraction** of the whole pizza. Fractions are pieces of a whole object.

Fractions

A fraction is made of three parts. The **denominator** is the number on the bottom. The **numerator** is the number on top. The line in the middle is the **fraction line**, or fraction bar.

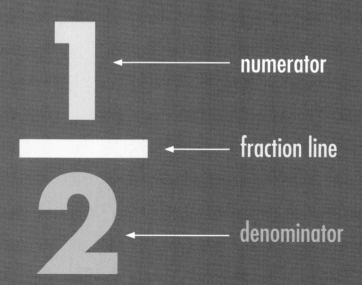

1 ← numerator

fraction line ←

2 ← denominator

The denominator tells how many total pieces something is divided into. The numerator tells how many of those pieces you have. When the pizza is cut into two pieces, the denominator is 2. If you have just one of the two pieces, the numerator is 1. $\frac{1}{2}$ means that you have 1 of 2 equal parts.

Here are some other common fractions:

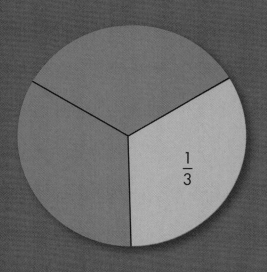

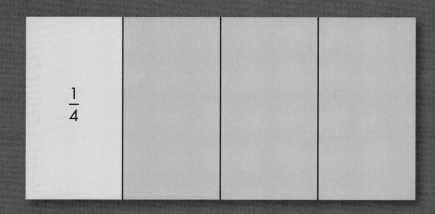

3
More Pizza

Ding-dong. Another pizza?

No, four more friends.

Now the pizza is divided into six equal pieces. Each slice is one-sixth of the whole pizza. One-sixth is written like this: $\frac{1}{6}$.

One friend is not hungry. This means another friend gets two of the six pieces, or $\frac{2}{6}$ of the whole pizza. Who gets more, a friend with $\frac{2}{6}$ of the pizza or a friend with $\frac{1}{6}$? If you ate $\frac{6}{6}$, you would eat the whole pizza!

$\frac{2}{6} =$

$= \frac{1}{6}$

4
Time for Dessert

Now it is time for dessert. One chocolate bar, six friends.

Ding-dong. Make that eight friends! One chocolate bar, eight pieces.

Which piece is bigger, one that is $\frac{1}{6}$ of the chocolate bar or one that is $\frac{1}{8}$ of the chocolate bar?

5

Fractions and Money

Knowing about fractions is helpful when we are sharing pizza and chocolate. What about when we are buying those things? **Money** can be described with fractions too.

A **quarter** is $\frac{1}{4}$ of a dollar.

A **dime** is $\frac{1}{10}$ of a dollar.

A **nickel** is $\frac{1}{20}$ of a dollar.

A **penny** is $\frac{1}{100}$ of a dollar.

You and your brother help a neighbor rake leaves. The neighbor gives you two quarters. That is $\frac{2}{4}$ of a dollar. Your brother gets five dimes. That is $\frac{5}{10}$ of a dollar. Who gets more money?

6

Fractions and Time

Time is also counted in fractions. There are 60 **minutes** in an **hour**.

How many minutes are in $\frac{1}{2}$ hour?

How many minutes are in $\frac{1}{4}$ hour?

You are given $\frac{1}{2}$ of an hour to read at bedtime. Your sister is given $\frac{1}{4}$ of an hour to read at bedtime. Who gets more time to read at bedtime?

Everyday Fractions

Fractions are everywhere. There are fractions in the kitchen.

There are fractions in the sky.

Best of all, there are delicious fractions to eat!

Glossary

denominator number below the fraction line. It shows the total number of portions.

dime coin that is worth 10 cents

fraction number that represents a portion of a whole

fraction line horizontal line that divides the numerator and denominator in a fraction

hour unit of time made up of 60 minutes

minute unit of time made up of 60 seconds

money coins or paper accepted as payment

nickel coin that is worth 5 cents

numerator number above the fraction line. It shows how many parts of the whole you have.

penny coin that is worth 1 cent

quarter coin that is worth 25 cents

Index